POCKE

Around Brecon

Drinkers having a pint at the White Swan in Llanfrynach, *c.* 1960. From left to right: the landlord of the Travellers Rest in Talybont-on-Usk, Noel Jones who was the landlord of the White Swan, Bill Williams landlord of the Markets Tavern in Brecon, Bill Griffiths and Penry Davies (Ty Mawr).

POCKET IMAGES

Around Brecon

Mike Davies
in association with
Gwyn Evans

NONSUCH

'The Family XI': a photograph taken in front of Ely Cottage in Brecon, c. 1860.

First published 2000
This new pocket edition 2005
Images unchanged from first edition

Nonsuch Publishing Limited
The Mill, Brimscombe Port,
Stroud, Gloucestershire, GL5 2QG
www.nonsuch-publishing.com

© Mike Davies, 2000

The right of Mike Davies to be identified as the Author
of this work has been asserted in accordance with the
Copyrights, Designs and Patents Act 1988.

British Library Cataloguing in Publication Data.
A catalogue record for this book is available from the British Library.

ISBN 1-84588-131-1

Typesetting and origination by Nonsuch Publishing Limited
Printed in Great Britain by Oaklands Book Services Limited

Contents

A B C D E F G H I K L M N O P Q R S T V

A Castell lane
B Old Port infer
C Old Port Super
D Canterceley Wa
E Shepe street
F High street Su
G High stret isf
H Lone y Poply
I Morganok Wa
K S. Marys Ward
L Llanua∫e Wa
M The Priory
N S. Iohn Evange
O S. Maryes Chap
P West gate
Q Watter gate
R North gate
S East gate
T Watton Ward
V Rewred Ward

BREKNOKE

50 100 150

A Scale of Pa∫es

A detail taken from Christopher Saxton Lea's map of South Wales of around 1580, gives a view of Brecon, showing the castle and priory, the streets and houses within the town walls, and the gardens and orchards outside the walls.

The ancient dug-out boat that was found in Llangorse Lake in 1925. Llangorse Lake is the largest natural lake in South Wales. Its man-made island, or crannog, has been dated to around AD 800 and it is thought that the boat relates to this period of settlement. The boat is now in Brecknock Museum.

Introduction

I have always been fascinated by the old county of Breconshire. I was born in a small village called Princetown on the edge of the 'Heads of the Valleys' of south-east Wales. Near Princetown, the River Rhymney marks the borderline between the three old counties of Glamorganshire, Monmouthshire and Breconshire. To the south is industrial Wales with some of the signs of coal mining and iron working still apparent in the highly populated valleys. To the north are the Brecon Beacons and rural Wales. I was always intrigued by the fact that part of Princetown was once in the parish of Llangynidr, in old Breconshire, and that there were old routes through the mountains that would lead to the Usk Valley in a much more direct line than could be achieved by car.

The villages and towns of Breconshire were popular locations for day trips when I was growing up. As a family we would often go to Brecon to visit the playground near the river and enjoy a picnic or a boat ride. When I learnt to drive I began to explore the area in much more detail. Llangorse Lake was always one of my favourite places to visit and I was overjoyed when my family decided to move to the village in 1993. I am proud to say that Llangorse is now very much my home. It is a unique place and I am continually overwhelmed by the friendliness and generosity of its people.

Brecon is the nearest major town to Llangorse and has a remarkable history. It recently celebrated its 900th anniversary, recognising the foundation of the town following the victory in 1093 of the Norman, Bernard de Neufmarche, over the Welsh leader Rhys ap Tewdwr. The battle site is thought to be at the point where the river Honddu meets the river Usk, and Bernard established a church (now the cathedral) in tribute, copying William the Conqueror's construction of Battle Abbey at Hastings.

Following de Neufmarche's conquest of the region, the town that quickly sprang up around his castle soon obtained borough status. In 1246 it was granted its borough charter, and by the mid-sixteenth century had become one of the most important towns in Wales.

The Brecon region takes its name from a famous Dark Age ruler called Brychan Brycheiniog, although the history of the Brecon district goes back much further than the foundation of the town or even Brychan himself. There is an imposing Iron Age fort at Pen-y-Crug, and the remains of what was once an important Roman fort (Y Gaer) just north of the present town.

The street layout of modern Brecon follows closely the original medieval plan, although much of the architecture is Georgian as the town became a fashionable winter resort for the rich in the eighteenth century. The town has undergone many significant changes in recent years. These changes include the building of the Theatre Brycheiniog, a waterside theatre which seats 400, Bethel Square, a new shopping precinct that incorporates some of the town's old buildings, while the old livestock market has been moved to an out of town site to make way for a supermarket development.

I am grateful for the opportunity to write this book. It has allowed me to learn much more about a district that is now my home and to meet people with a shared interest in its history. I would like to pay special thanks to Gwyn Evans, without whose assistance the production of this book would have been difficult, if not impossible. Gwyn is very well known in Brecon and his bookshop is a treasure trove for those with an interest in local history. His knowledge of the town and his incredible photograph collection, to which he kindly granted me access, made my task much more straightforward and enjoyable.

Mike Davies
March 2000

The priory church of St John the Evangelist, now Brecon Cathedral.

One

Pastimes

The cast of a production of Island Fling at the Brecon Little Theatre, the Watton, in April 1938. Brecon has an important theatrical history dating back to before 1700 and the new waterside theatre complex at the head of the canal basin, opened in 1996, continues this tradition into the new millennium. The town was the birthplace of the internationally renowned eighteenth-century actress Sarah Siddons.

A Sunday school children's tea party taking place at Brecon Market Hall, *c.* 1935.

Brecon Grammar School prefects, 1949/50. In the photograph are L.V.G. Jones, L. Hargest, W.J. Price, John Fouely (?), H.A.J. Butler, J.K. Jones, Glyn Powell, David W. Rice, B. Grant, and David Candy.

Mrs Basset's 1946 class from Mount Street School, out on a nature ramble near Ty'n y Cae with teacher Vic Jones who took this photograph.

The Priory Groves in the cathedral grounds.

A children's party entitled 'Tea in the Market' taking place at Brecon Market Hall in 1935.

The sprinters dip for the line in the final of the 100 yards race at Brecon Sports Ground, the Watton, around 1954.

People playing on the frozen surface of the river Usk at Brecon on 17 January 1946.

Brecon Table Tennis Club receiving prizes in 1939. From left to right, back row: Jack Coppt, Arthur Hill, David Jenkins, Vic Jones. Front row: S. Jenkins, Mrs Jolly, Les Hargest, Mr Jolly, Ralph Page. The club played in a room above what is now the post office next to St Mary's church.

Brecon 1st Scout Group pictured in 1945.

Young Wales Club, Brecon c. 1940. This club used to meet in Dr Coke's Hall, part of the old Methodist chapel founded by Dr Coke which once stood near the site of the present-day Co-op.

A boxing booth set up outside Eastman's and Ross & Sons in Brecon High Street, c. 1945. Fairs have been an important part of Brecon life ever since the town's charter, granted in 1246, allowed it to hold both markets and fairs. Originally fairs were an important way for traders to meet and exchange goods and were often specialized, such as the horse fairs in Llanfaes. As communications improved in the late nineteenth century the purpose of fairs became more and more for entertainment with booths and side-shows filling the streets.

A canal outing photographed near Watton Villa, c. 1910. Canal outings were very popular in Brecon, particularly with the Sunday schools who would often take a trip to Brynich Lock Field where sports and games were organized.

A Sunday school canal trip, c. 1910. The Brecon and Abergavenny Canal was opened in 1800 and extended to Pontypool in 1811. Before the advent of steam power it was an important trade link and was constructed because of the need to move items such as coal, limestone and lime in exchange for agricultural goods. On the far side of the canal is Charles Street, just off the Watton.

A number of well-dressed ladies can be seen on a canal barge being led under one of the bridges on the way to Brynich Lock.

A group of Sunday School members competing in an egg and spoon race in Brynich Lock Field around 1910.

A group of children in fancy dress at Llangorse carnival on VJ Day, August 1945.

Brecon Cycling Club on an excursion in 1894. It is noticeable from the photograph that this appears to be a male membership only club. The club was founded at the Royal Hart Refreshment Rooms in the Watton in May 1890.

Passengers and passers-by stop what they are doing to be photographed outside the Fountain Inn, Ship Street (now the Workmen's Club), c. 1890.

Motorcycles from the Brecon and Radnor Motorcycle Club lined up outside the Wellington Hotel for the start of a reliability trial in 1912. Note the cobbled surface of the road and the EU prefixes on many of the machines' numberplates. At this time EU was the prefix for vehicles from Breconshire.

A car driving towards the Storey Arms on the Brecon to Merthyr road, c. 1935.

A later motorcycle reliability trial at Cradoc, *c.* 1935.

A Caravan Club rally driving along the Bulwark in Brecon, *c.* 1930.

The fly-half waits for the ball during a Christ College 1st XV rugby match, c. 1900. The college has a proud sporting heritage, and its 'local derby' matches with Llandovery College are always important fixtures.

An ox roast taking place in the grounds of Christ College in May 1931.

Brecon Hunt gathering outside the Castle Hotel, c. 1910. The caption on the card reads, 'Brecon Huntsmen, Off to meet the King', which means that they are off to chase the fox.

Brecon Classics (Junior) Football Club during its 1912/13 season.

The river Usk, Brecon, *c.* 1910. Bathing was a very popular pastime in the Edwardian era and ladies' changing rooms were constructed right on the banks of the river, pre-empting the development of a swimming-pool for local bathers. Note the full body swimming costumes the ladies are wearing to preserve their modesty.

Fenni Fach Rocks, *c.* 1900. The rocks, at the far end of the Promenade, were a very popular trysting place for young couples around this time.

Left: The huge bonfire constructed on Fenni Fach Hill to mark the Coronation of George VI in 1937. Brecon residents worked through the previous night to ensure that this enormous bonfire was ready in time to mark the occasion.

Below: People skating on the thick ice of the frozen River Usk in Brecon during the winter of 1963. Throughout this very severe winter children from outlying villages were kept out of school for many weeks.

Opposite above: The Watton, Brecon. A street party in full swing in Tom Cross's Yard to celebrate the end of the Second World War.

Opposite below: A crowd gathers outside the Palace Cinema at its opening in 1912. Perry's removal firm later used the building.

The Guild Hall in Brecon, c. 1935. Dance bands were a popular form of entertainment during this period and regularly visited the town, often playing at the Guild Hall.

A street party taking place outside the Markets Tavern on Free Street in 1945. The old livestock market can be seen in the background.

Above: A youth group pictured inside the Plough Chapel, Brecon, c. 1940. The current chapel stands on the site of the earliest Nonconformist chapel in Brecon.

Right: George and Barbara Harris photographed in their costumes as the Herald and the Fairy in Talybont-on-Usk school's production of Cinderella in January 1914.

Reginald Evans receiving the Northcote Cup for Talybont-on-Usk in 1937 at the old racecourse, near the gasworks in Brecon.

The winning team proudly displays the Northcote Cup and their individual medals.

A group of Brecon children in front of Elston's Garage and the old mill in the Struet, *c.* 1950.

A large Civic Sunday parade, *c.* 1900. The parade is pictured outside the priory church (now the cathedral) on its way into the Struet.

A group of Brecon people enjoying a day trip in a charabanc, c. 1925. These vehicles became a popular method of transport from the early 1900s onwards and were often based around a lorry chassis to allow room for large groups of people.

A very early automobile owned by the de Winton family, pictured here in 1905. Note the Breconshire numberplate of EU7.

An early automobile at Glan Usk Park, c. 1912. The BX numberplate is a Carmarthenshire prefix.

John Lloyd outside Dinas House with his two cars, EU945 and 'Sarah' the Sunbeam. The photograph dates from spring 1930. Lloyd founded the original museum in Glamorgan Street which was later re-established in the Shire Hall (its present site).

A children's Christmas party in Llanfrynach in the presence of local MP Capt. Hall of Abercynrig, *c.* 1936.

Two

Brecon Town

A gathering of the congregation, which includes Mrs Davies of Llandefaelog Cottage, at the Plough Chapel in 1938.

The two saddle tank locomotives of the midday Brecon to Merthyr train can be seen coupled to carriages and ready to leave Brecon station in this picture from around 1900. The Brecon to Merthyr line was opened to traffic on 1 May 1863 and immediately improved communication between rural mid-Wales and the rapidly expanding industrial areas of the South Wales valleys.

A view looking back towards the town from Brecon railway station shortly after its closure around 1964. The station was also known as Free Street station and there were other stations at the Watton and Mount Street.

Brecon railway station shortly after closure. The station was almost certainly closed due to the reforms implemented after Dr Beeching's report in the early 1960s. This is now the site of the modern fire station.

The turntable at Brecon railway station shortly after closure around 1964.

The dramatic ruins of the castle at Brecon, *c.* 1850. Building started in 1093, following the conquest of the area by Bernard de Neufmarche. It was later enlarged by the de Braose and de Bohun lords of Brecon. Much of the damage to the castle occurred during the English Civil War period in the seventeenth century.

The Castle Hotel around 1870, seen from Llanfaes Bridge at the point where two rivers, the Usk and the Honddu, meet. The original Honddu bridge was destroyed in a flood in 1853 and was replaced with the stone bridge visible in the right of the picture. This though was destroyed by another flood in 1873. In 1874 the present iron bridge was built in its place. There are three bridges across the Honddu – the Priory, Castle and Honddu bridges. Llanfaes Bridge crosses the river Usk and is the route into Brecon from the west. The importance of these bridges to the people of Brecon was demonstrated by the way that they contributed heavily to their upkeep.

A very early photograph of Christ College and chapel, c. 1850. In the medieval period, Christ College was a Dominican friary and was probably founded around 1250. The chapel dates from the same period and is an excellent example of a thirteenth-century building. In 1541 Henry VIII established a school here by royal charter while in 1855 the modern public school was established through an Act of Parliament.

Llanfaes Bridge and Christ College, c. 1850. Pen-y-Fan, the highest point in the Brecon Beacons, is just visible in the background.

The Bulwark in Brecon, c. 1945. On the left are the L-shaped seventeenth-century town houses that were re-fronted during the eighteenth century. Shop fronts were added during Victorian times. Note the imposing shape of St Mary's church in the background.

The priory church, c. 1850. An early exterior view of the building that was to become Brecon Cathedral in 1923. The first bishop for the diocese of Swansea and Brecon was Edward Latham Bevan.

The cathedral churchyard in the late nineteenth century.

In the foreground of this 1850s photograph of the priory church is the famous twelfth-century Norman font. In 1093, Bernard de Neufmarche, the conqueror of Brecheiniog, gave this church to a monk of Battle Abbey in Hastings. The grant led to the foundation of both a Benedictine priory and the church, which celebrated its 900th anniversary in 1993. The building was once noted as being the finest parish church in Wales and in 1923 was elevated to cathedral status when the Church in Wales was inaugurated.

The Bishop of Swansea and Brecon photographed with members of the clergy at Brecon Cathedral in 1997.

St Mary's church and the Wellington Hotel, *c.* 1865. Note the near deserted streets and absence even of any horse-drawn traffic.

A family photographed outside Ely Cottage sometime during the 1870s.

A late nineteenth-century portrait of a group of gentlemen outside Ely Cottage. They appear to be members of the same family that is pictured on page four of this book, making this a photograph of a father and four of his sons. In 1891 Kelly's Directory lists the residents of Ely Cottage as Thomas David William Evans and Thomas David William Jones.

'Ely Cottage Rookery': a late nineteenth-century photograph of the town with the rookery in the middle distance. This vantage point is now occupied by the houses of Bron-y-Crug, Dan-y-Crug, and the Uplands.

'Equipped for a drive': the children of Ely Cottage with their pet cat, pictured around 1865, about to go for a ride in their little donkey-drawn carriage.

Ely Cottage once occupied a site adjacent to the castle. However the building fell into disrepair in the twentieth century, was demolished and the new bishop's residence was built in its place.

This photograph of the bishop's residence, built on the site of Ely Cottage, provides a means of comparison and shows that although the building is different the overall shape of the gardens has remained relatively unchanged.

Newton Farm, Brecon, has origins in the sixteenth century and was the home of the famous Breconshire family, the Games. The most infamous member of this family was Dafydd Gam who fought, and died, at the battle of Agincourt in 1415. Prior to this he was outlawed for killing one of his relatives, Richard Fawr of Slwch, in Brecon High Street. He was a famous opponent of Owain Glyn Dwr and his exploits ensured that he was the only Brecon person to be mentioned in a Shakespearean play, as Fluellen in Henry IV.

An aerial photograph of Brecon taken during the 1950s.

The river Honddu, Brecon.

The Honddu mill pictured with Brecon Castle in the background, *c.* 1875. The mill-wheel has long since disappeared .

The flooding of the river Usk around Christ College, c. 1880. It is possible to see that the water has risen almost to the doors of the main college building.

Timber haulage horses can be seen here being led along the Bulwark past St Mary's church around 1925.

Ship Street, Brecon, c. 1950. Men would gather here to be available for work. Note the exposed timber framing of the building occupied by Mayall's the silversmiths (since demolished).

Left: A very early photograph of Brecon Guild Hall in High Street Inferior, *c.* 1840. The first town hall was built by John Abel of Herefordshire in 1624. It was re-structured in 1770 and, in the early nineteenth century, consisted of a large court-house on the first floor above an open market-place with stalls in the vaults. The attic was used to store armaments for the local regiment until the building of the armoury in the Watton in 1805.

Below: This photograph was taken from outside Lloyds Bank in the High Street around 1930, looking towards the Bulwark. Note the Games' water fountain and lamp-post which were removed from the centre of High Street Inferior in 1934.

BRECON, BIRTH PLACE OF SARAH SIDDONS

The man in the left of the picture outside the Sarah Siddons pub is the famous British playwright, George Bernard Shaw (1856-1950). Sarah Siddons was a world renowned actress who was born in the Shoulder of Mutton pub (which now bears her name) on 5 July 1755. To the right are the premises of the former Brecon Old Bank, taken over by Lloyds Bank in 1890.

People gathered outside the original market place in Brecon High Street, *c.* 1860. Originally the Guild Hall combined the functions of a borough and market hall. In 1888 it was rebuilt and the ground-floor corn market was converted into a council chamber, borough police court, mayor's parlour and town clerk's office.

Union Jacks are flying in High Street Superior in 1937 to celebrate the Coronation of George VI. The market hall is on the right.

A drawing from around 1840 looking down Ship Street, showing just how narrow it was with its half-timbered buildings and late-medieval houses.

A view looking up Ship Street towards the High Street, c. 1900. Most of the buildings to the left have since been demolished, and the library now stands in their place.

The Struet in Brecon, c. 1900. The shop on the right is now Gwyn Evans' bookshop and the Angel Hotel is now the RAFA Club.

A view looking towards Watton Mount, that dates from around 1900, with the tower of St Mary's church in the background. The Watton was an early suburb of Brecon that developed during the Georgian and Regency periods as the town became a fashionable winter resort for the rich.

Right: A large number of people have turned out to have their picture taken in this photograph of Lion Street, *c.* 1900.

Below: Construction work taking place prior to the widening of Watton Pitch Road, *c.* 1923. The Shire Hall, on the left of the picture, was designed by Thomas Wyatt and David Brandon and was built in 1842. The Breconshire quarter sessions were held here until 1972 before the building began its new role as the Brecknock Museum in 1974.

Promenade, Brecknock.

Above: A view looking down the tree-lined Promenade around 1900, while a young boy takes a rest on a bench. Just visible in the distance is the town centre, dominated by the tower of St Mary's church.

Left: Jack Jenkins (also known as 'Jack the Rollerman') walking down the Watton in the direction of the barracks with the Gremlin Hotel in the foreground and the Camden Arms on the opposite side of the road. The line of trees is part of a group of twenty-four lime trees planted along the Watton in recognition of the achievements of the 24th Foot, South Wales Borderers.

Brecon, The Barracks.

Above: Brecon gradually became an important military centre during the nineteenth century. In 1805 an armaments store was built in the Watton, which formed the basis for the barracks that were built between 1842 and 1844. In 1881 the barracks became the permanent HQ for the South Wales Borderers who were immortalized at the battle of Rorke's Drift, later recalled in the film *Zulu* (see page 126).

Right: Two men pose solemnly on the King Charles Steps at the end of the Struet, *c.* 1890. It is claimed that the steps were given their name after King Charles I ran up them to escape from Parliamentarians during the Civil War.

A picture of the old railway bridge, taken from the drawing-room of Priory Hill House on 24 July 1933. It is possible to see a series of sheds or workshops in the arches underneath the bridge.

A different view of the old railway bridge in which more of the buildings next to the railway can be seen. The bridge went across the Struet and over the River Honddu at this point.

Three

Events

Prize winners in the dog show at Brecon Agricultural Show in 1936.

An infants' class and their teachers at Mount Street School in 1902. Education was made compulsory for children in 1870 and schools such as Mount Street were built to cope with the rising demand for places.

Interested crowds gather round to look at the rifles left outside Brecon Cathedral during a military service in 1925.

A harsh winter in 1920 causing the urgent repair of street lighting in Brecon High Street. The workmen's job must have been made particularly difficult by the continuing heavy snowfall.

Brecon Market Hall on 8 September 1923. The Liberal leader David Lloyd-George is pictured leaving the hall after finishing a speech. He was granted the freedom of the borough in a presentation by the mayor. A large crowd had gathered outside the hall waiting to catch a glimpse of the former Prime Minister.

Brecon Recreation Ground, c. 1950. A summer festival featuring a children's parade with the carnival queen and her attendants. The old Brecon gasworks is visible in the background.

Brecon residents pictured during one of the town's many floods, c. 1925.

Stranded residents in Bridge Street clamber into a rescue boat during severe flooding of the river Usk around 1960, while other residents waiting to be rescued look on from their upstairs windows.

Bridge Street leading to Llanfaes, Brecon, *c.* 1960. The same rescue boat, by now full of people, makes its way down the road past the Christ College playing-fields on the left.

Bronllys, 17 July 1920. The visit of King George V and Queen Mary to mark the official opening of the newly completed South Wales Sanatorium.

Brecknockshire Agricultural Society, 6 August 1955. Officials being presented to Queen Elizabeth II and Prince Philip at the bicentenary show.

A group of Brecon ladies on their way to a political gathering, pictured in the Bulwark, c. 1928. Note where the driver of the charabanc is sitting – he is in the middle of the front row of seats and the vehicle has a central steering-column. The sign on the side of the charabanc reads 'Liberalism means practical ways to better days'.

A military procession of the 1st Battalion of the South Wales Borderers on the way to Brecon Cathedral on 1 April 1934. The procession was to mark the laying up of Colours in the old Havard Chapel in the cathedral. In the First World War this regiment lost 5,777 men, and in the Second World War, 1,025 men. The South Wales Borderers are commemorated in the chapel today.

Union Jacks adorn the buildings in the High Street to mark a national event, probably the Coronation of George VI in May 1937.

The Struet, Brecon, c. 1937. More flags in the streets, again most probably to mark the Coronation of George VI. The old railway bridge, visible in the background of the picture, was dismantled in 1964 after the closure of the railway station.

The mayor of Brecon pictured with town officials at the Civic Sunday parade in the Struet, *c.* 1920.

Escort to the Assize Judge outside County House in the Struet, *c.* 1960. Following the Acts of Union in 1536 and 1543, Brecon became the venue for the Great Sessions and Quarter Sessions. In 1831 the Great Sessions were replaced by the South Wales assize circuit. Under this system an Assize Judge would visit the town twice a year to hear major criminal cases. The system continued until 1971 when it was replaced with the current legal system.

The Assize Judge and court officials pictured in 1970 with the father and son team of Assize Trumpeters, Mr Reg Williams of John Street and his son Peter.

A packed High Street can be seen here as a huge Civic Sunday parade returns from a service at the priory church (now the cathedral), c. 1900.

The Plough Chapel choir, c. 1940.

A Mothers' Union procession making its way along the Bulwark, c. 1925.

The Civic Sunday parade outside the Landsdowne Hotel in the Watton, *c.* 1900.

Priory School, Brecon, *c.* 1935.

Members of the military proudly displaying a captured German gun to Brecon townspeople at the height of the First World War, on 31 March 1916. Displays such as this were fairly common during the war in a bid to boost the morale of a nation disillusioned with the war it had been predicted would be 'over by Christmas'.

A children's procession along Brecon High Street around 1920.

Soldiers returning from the First World War in 1919: the crowds have gathered to watch them marching past Bowen Terrace into Free Street.

A party of ATC cadets in an RAF bomber dinghy on the river Usk during a 'Wings for Victory' promotion in 1943. In the dinghy with Mayor Parry de Winton are cadets Price, Brookes, Morgan, Russel, Coombe, Priday, and Williams.

Brecon Livestock Market, 1999. Brecon has been allowed to hold regular markets, by town charter, for almost as long as the town has existed. Recent redevelopment of the town centre has led to the controversial decision to move the market from its traditional site in the centre of town to an out of town site. The original market site is now part of a new supermarket development.

Brecon Livestock Market, 1999. This was the very last market before the site was moved to an out of town development, so marking the end of centuries of tradition.

A children's tea-party taking place in a crowded Brecon Market Hall, *c.* 1920.

The ancient Roman ruins at Gaer Camp near Cradoc, Brecon. Excavations can be seen taking place here on the remains of the fort's granary. The camp was one of the key Roman positions in this part of Britain.

Residents gather round to look at the overhead lines that have been brought down by severe snow and ice around 1940.

A class of pupils from Mount Street School, pictured here with their teachers in 1914.

Children and staff of Mount Street School seen here in 1914.

Mount Street School staff including **Mr Winstanley** (headmaster), Horace Norman, Vic Jones, Miss Hargest, Phyllis Davies and Don Davies, in this photograph from around 1928.

Mount Street School staff in 1936. From left to right, back row: Angelo Adami, Olwen Evans, Vic Jones. Front row: Betty Armstrong, -?-, Mr Grant, Phyllis Davies, Miss Stubbs.

Members of the Brecon Rotary Club photographed outside the Castle Hotel, Brecon, on the formation of the club in 1959.

Members of Brecon Rotary Club pictured outside the Castle Hotel in 1995.

Residents of the cottages in Dinas Road look out on the floodwaters during another one of the river Usk's floods. These cottages, pictured here around 1900, used to be flooded regularly and have since been demolished. The area is now a car park off Bridge Street.

Ty Mawr, Llanfrynach, c. 1890. The de Winton family carriage, with its immaculately groomed horses and smart footman and driver, waits outside their residence.

A Pickford's truck negotiating a heavy load through the narrow entrance to Ship Street in 1950 while two men look on, apparently puzzled as to how the truck is going to fit through such a narrow gap.

A dramatic picture of the same truck, seemingly still stuck in the same position in Ship Street, emphasizing the difficulties faced by heavy traffic making its way through the town prior to road widening and the construction of the bypass.

Brecon High Street Inferior in 1995. The Brecon Jazz Festival has become an annual event of great significance to the town since its inception in 1984.

An automobile, possibly a delivery van, overturned and lying half submerged in the Brecon canal outside the old slaughterhouse. It appears that a number of workers from the slaughterhouse have come out to examine the stricken vehicle.

A chauffeur waiting for his employer outside the Wellington Hotel, c. 1912.

A well-to-do couple in their chauffeur-driven limousine outside the Castle Hotel, c. 1920. The hotel was established by the Morgan family of Tredegar House near Newport in the early 1800s, and became a popular coaching inn.

Four

Trades and Occupations

Workers and officials involved in the restoration of the Brecon Cathedral precincts around 1926-1927.

Breconshire Home Guard during the Second World War consisted of the men of Brecon, Talybont, Llanwern, Llangorse and Llanfihangel districts. Pictured on the far right, second row from the top is Mr Reginald Evans, formerly of Talybont and later Llanfihangel.

Soldiers in procession crossing the bridge in Castle Street, Brecon, c. 1910.

School canteen staff in Brecon pictured during 1946.

Above: The Fountain Inn at the bottom of Ship Street, *c*. 1900. The site of the inn is now occupied by the Workmen's Club.

Left: An advertisement for Meredith & Stanton, chemists, which was on the corner of the High Street and Castle Street. The poster proudly boasts that the shop had a 'convenient dark-room for customers' as well as offering developing and printing for amateurs. This was later the site, for many years, of Boots the Chemist, before its move to Bethel Square.

Opposite above: The Brecon Show, *c*. 1920. J. E. Nott and Co. and other exhibitors at the show ground.

Opposite below: A display of American tractors outside the Modern Garage in Brecon (Elston's in the Struet), *c*. 1917. Due to a shortage of horses for farm work, the tractors were loaned by the military for use by local farmers as part of the war effort.

Larkin & Company,

General and Fancy Drapers.
Milliners, Dressmakers,
Ladies and Gent.'s Outfitters & Tailors,

25, High Street, BRECON.

Military Uniforms.

Riding Breeches and Liveries a Speciality.

Mourning Orders promptly attended to.

Larkin & Co., drapers, of High Street, Brecon. This store was opposite the entrance to the Market Hall and is now occupied by Buds & Blooms.

Morris' tobacconists and grocers shop in Bridge Street, Brecon, c. 1900. It is possible that the man standing in the shop doorway is Mr Morris.

John Hando Ltd, of No. 18 High Street, Brecon. The sign above the door of the jeweller's and watchmaker's says 'Contractors to the War Department' and 'Midland and Cambrian Railways'.

The Brecon shopkeepers' exhibition at the Brecon Show, *c.* 1920.

Cynog Jones, an outfitter's which was situated opposite St Mary's church in Brecon High Street, c. 1900.

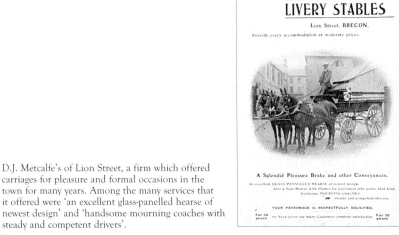

D.J. Metcalfe's of Lion Street, a firm which offered carriages for pleasure and formal occasions in the town for many years. Among the many services that it offered were 'an excellent glass-panelled hearse of newest design' and 'handsome mourning coaches with steady and competent drivers'.

Cash & Co. shoe shop which was on the corner of High Street and Ship Street, c. 1920. The site is now occupied by Lovely Things.

Ship Street, Brecon, c. 1910. This general store would later become, for many years, the premises of the West Breconshire Farmers' Store.

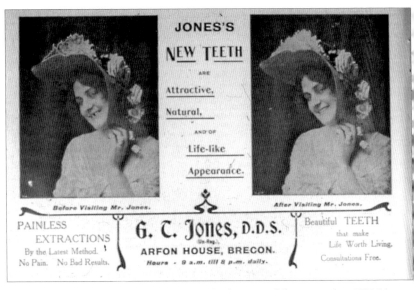

An advertisement by G. C. Jones of Arfon House for dentures and dentistry work, c. 1900. Mr Jones offered a wide variety of dentistry work but seemed to specialize in his own type of repair work promising to give customers 'beautiful teeth that make life worth living'.

High Street, Brecon. Pictured is F. James the decorators merchant's, a shop now occupied by Motor World.

Above: Central Garage which sold petrol at the bottom of Ship Street. The advertisement on the side of the building shows passing motorists that it has parts for many different types of car including Morris, Humber and Hillman. At one time the Central Garage had two showrooms in Brecon. (Photograph by Stanley P. Rowlands)

Right: Sullivan's the ironmongers that was situated in Bridge Street, Brecon. The photograph dates from around 1935.

THOMAS & ADCOCK,

General and Fancy Drapers, Mantlemen and Furriers

Warwick House, BRECON.

First-class Dress-making and Millinery

Noted for Household Linens.

An advertisement for Thomas & Adcock's shop in Warwick House, now Clarke's toyshop.

David Morgan

Tailor and Draper, Brecon

Agent for Dr. Jaeger's Under-clothing.

David Morgan's, the tailors and drapers shop that was once in the High Street, pictured here around 1900. These premises are now occupied by Peacock's.

Right: Poulston's hairdressing salon on the corner of Castle Street and the Struet, c. 1890. The shop is now Knight's Rentals.

Below: Construction workers building the reservoir at Talybont-on-Usk in 1925. The shed in the background belonged to the contractor, Ben Jones of Sketty.

A landmark event for Brecon as electricity is introduced to the town at Elston's Garage in the Struet around 1925. A great many townspeople have turned out to view the event.

Bystanders view the aftermath of the fire on 3 June 1936 that completely gutted Brecon Motors on the Watton.

On the roof of the Midland Bank in Brecon High Street. These workmen are pictured on the completion of building work around 1900.

Repairs being carried out on the bridge over the River Honddu on Castle Street. The picture was taken around 1960.

A group of workers outside the old slaughterhouse in Canal Road, near Captain's Walk, c. 1935.

Some of the fine animals to be shown at Brecon's famous horse fair in Bridge Street, c. 1935. The fair took place outside the old wool factory and near to the site of the present day surgery. Usk House is in the background.

Huge crowds throng Bridge Street at the horse fair, c. 1935.

Breconshire Home Guard pictured during the Second World War. These mounted soldiers are thought to be from the area around Dyffryn Crawnon and Llangynidr.

Nurses and young patients pictured in one of the large and well-lit wards of Craig-y-Nos hospital, *c.* 1910. In the late nineteenth century this house was the home of the famous opera singer Adelena Patti.

Nurses from Brecon War Memorial Hospital, pictured around 1940 with children from a first aid class.

A happy group of railway staff photographed at Brecon railway station, c. 1940.

Policemen and firemen pass County House on the Struet as part of a Civic Sunday parade, c. 1925.

Post Office employees posing for a group photograph outside the old post office in Lion Street around 1900. The building later became the showroom of Brooke's Central Garage.

A group of firemen pictured with their horse-drawn Merryweather appliance in the Postern around 1910.

A slightly later photograph of firemen posing alongside their, now motorized, appliance outside the Castle Hotel, around 1920.

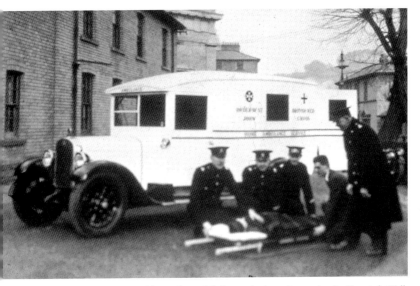

A St John's Ambulance crew holding a first-aid drill outside the police station in Captain's Walk in 1935.

The butcher's boy: a horse and trap making deliveries for Eastman's of Brecon, *c.* 1900.

Five

Around Brecon

Roger Jones (Ty Fry) and Ted Jones stop for a chat outside the post office in Llanfrynach in 1962.

Drinkers in the White Swan, Llanfrynach, enjoying a pint and a game of cards around 1960.
From left: Ivor Phillips, Jack Pugh, 'Jumbo' Edwards and Dennis Watkins.

Jim Preece playing the one-armed-bandit in the White Swan, Llanfrynach, c. 1962.

Llanfrynach School, 1962/63. Staff: Morgan Gronnow (headmaster), Margaret Meyrick (teacher).
Children, from left to right, back row: Mervyn Jones (Llwyn Ron), Derrick Evans, Ron Watkins,
Sandra Davies, Janet Chapell, Kathleen Jarman, John Davies, Dai Morgan, Terry Watkins. Middle
row: Phillip Price, Peter Naylor, Eleanor Lewis, Barbara Lewis, Barry Thomas, Martin Evans, Tony
Watkins, Robin Naylor, Penny Naylor, Angela Thomas, Jean Morgan. Front row: Jackie Pugh,
Gethin Watkins, Keith Evans, Lindsey Price, Dulcie Davies.

A group of Llangorse children in fancy dress for the Empire Day carnival in 1940.

Above: Charabancs on a day outing to Llangorse Lake around 1930, stopping at the Red Lion in Llangorse for refreshments.

Left: The Red Lion Hotel, Llangorse, *c.* 1940. Proud fishermen displaying their impressive catches of pike after a day's fishing at Llangorse Lake. The lake has always attracted sports fishermen and is famous for its large pike.

A group of children sitting on the wall between Llangorse School and St Paulinus' church in 1953. Fifth from the left is Mrs Ann Gray who loaned the photograph.

A group of children ready to push off at Llangorse Lake in July 1932. The lake was, and still is, a popular destination for day trippers and holiday-makers. Pictured in the rear of the boat, holding the oar, is William Partridge Davies (1871–1958) whose family still hires boats out at the lake today.

William Partridge Davies, pictured around 1955 at Llangorse Lake.

Llangorse (noted for its Lake)

A postman standing outside the old post office in Llangorse around 1890. The view is of the road leading out of the village towards Bwlch.

Main Road in Llangorse, *c.* 1890. In the picture is the Castle Inn with the old school visible behind it. On the opposite side of the road is the Penuel Baptist Chapel which has stood in the heart of the village since 1869, closing for worship in 1996.

A view of Llangorse Common from the jetty on the lake: a traditional fair, with merry-go-round, swing-boats and other attractions has been set up, and there is a large marquee in the distance.

Left: St Paulinus' church, Llangorse, *c.* 1880. This medieval church has Dark Age origins and relics from the eighth century have been discovered on the site. It is believed that this may have been the site of an early Christian monastery.

Below: Peterstone Court, Llanhamlach, *c.* 1890. The house took its name from the adjacent church of St Peter. It has medieval origins although the original house was demolished when it passed from the Walbeoffe family to the Powells. The present building dates from 1741 and Lord Glanusk later owned the house. The court is now a hotel and health spa.

A steam-engine pictured exiting the tunnel at Tal-y-Llyn, *c.* 1960.

Tal-y-Llyn railway station, *c.* 1960. The old refreshment rooms are visible in the background along with a Rhymney Breweries sign. The rooms were a popular meeting place for local drinkers with the railway providing a useful link to other hostelries.

A group of farmers photographed with their dogs in Upper Chapel around 1965.

Aber Road, Talybont·on·Usk. 2605.

A group of children standing in front of some battered looking goal-posts in Aber Road, Talybont-on-Usk in the 1910s.

'The Haymakers': this float with its magnificent shire-horse took part in the carnival at Talybont-on-Usk in 1942.

Talybont-on-Usk, c. 1936. A group of children pictured in fancy dress, some of whom have even decorated their bicycles. The boy with the fox's head on his bicycle is Reginald Evans.

A huge crowd has turned out to watch a balloon begin its ascent at Buckland Fête around 1900.

A section of the crowd watching the balloon ascent at Buckland Fête.

A postcard showing Talybont-on-Usk from the canal around 1935. The sender of the card has written to her mother asking her to meet her off the No. 5 tram at the station.

Two lads standing in the road at Crossoak in Talybont-on-Usk.

The GWR bus stopping to pick up passengers at Bwlch. Since there was no direct railway link, the bus provided a connection between the stations at Brecon and Abergavenny from places such as Bwlch and Crickhowell.

Sennybridge pictured in the early twentieth century.

A pannier tank engine with a full head of steam pulling out of Torpantau station, *c.* 1960.

Staff pictured both on and off the platform at Talgarth railway station, *c.* 1900.

Penpont, c. 1860. This is one of the great old houses of Breconshire and it is currently undergoing extensive restoration following many years of decay. A huge oak timber cut from the Penpont estate was used to make a beam to support 'Big Ben' at the Houses of Parliament around 1895. Timber haulage horses belonging to Brown's Hauliers of Defynnog transported the timber to Brecon railway station. During the transfer to the station, a wheel came off the timber-carriage and the load blocked Ship Street for several days.

Six

Brecon and the New Millennium

Brecon Leisure Centre and Sports Ground, 1998. The new leisure centre was among the first of a series of improvements to the fabric of the town. Some of the changes have been controversial but Brecon continues to develop as a thriving town while retaining its links with its important historical past.

The Mid and West Wales Fire Service with Gwyn Evans (helicopter pilot) and the winner of a helicopter ride through the Brecon Beacons as part of a charity drive.

Brecon Leisure Centre staff, 1999. From left to right: Steve Davies, Jemma Williams, Dale Jackman, Matthew Jones, Kirsty Evans, Richard Dingley, Martin Scott, Edward Dyer, Richard Breslin, Danny Holinger, Peter Tracy, Kath Evans, Eddie Bolter.

Brecon general practitioners, outside Ty Henry Vaughan, Bridge Street, 1999. From left to right: Dr Musa, Dr Wrench, Dr Ricketts, Dr Johnson, Dr Faulkner, Dr Dimyan, Chris Johnson (Practice Manager), Dr A Davies (Senior Partner), Dr Heneghan, Dr Williams, Dr Bacon, Dr D. Davies.

The South Wales Borderers Museum staff, 1999. From left to right: Lucy Jones, Martin Everett, Celia Green. The museum, at the barracks, celebrates the history of the regiment including one of the most famous victories in British military history when 140 men of the South Wales Borderers defended the small outpost of Rorke's Drift against 4,000 Zulu warriors. Thanks to their bravery they suffered only a few casualties and eleven men were awarded the Victoria Cross – the highest accolade in the British armed forces.

Theatre Brycheiniog staff, 1999. The theatre was opened by Prince Charles on 29 July 1997 and is the latest in a series of Brecon buildings associated with theatre productions, dating back to the eighteenth century.

Brecknock Museum staff, 1999. Back row, from left to right: Martin Williams, David Moore (Curator), Malcolm Johns. Front row: Ann Blake, Caroline Hamilton, Julia Phillips, Meg Keeble. The museum is housed in the town's former court-house.

Brecon Library staff, 1999. From left to right: Sue Jones, Delyth Eckley, Chris Price, Kath Vause, Mark Jones, Ann Roberts.

Acknowledgements

I have already mentioned the role played by Gwyn Evans in the production of this book and his assistance and the quality of his photographic collection have been of great importance. I would like to thank my brother, Sean, for his excellent editorial skills and practical advice as well as my partner Julie and my parents, Jim and Monica, for their help in organizing the material. Alongside these I would like to thank Martin Evans, of Llangorse, for his assistance in dating key pictures and in sourcing pictures from the villages around Llanfrynach, as well as Michael and Melanie Tunnicliffe, Ray and Wendy Davies, and Garnett and Nina Davies (all of Lakeside, Llangorse) for their insight into the history of the lake and their family links to it. I am also grateful to Rob and Anne Gray for their photographs and support in the project.

I would like to thank the following for their assistance, either in donating pictures for the book or in practical ways relating to the compilation of the material or their invaluable local knowledge: Meurig and Elizabeth Evans of Llanfrynach, Carol Evans of Llangorse, Mrs Blanch Evans of Llanfihangel Tal-y-Llyn, Trevor Clark, Keith Morris, Ken Jones (Chairman of the Brecknock Society), Paul Holland of Cardiff, Tony Gregory of Tredegar, Jeanette Arnold of Llanfihangel Tal-y-Llyn. I wish to thank the many other people who offered pictures that I was unable to include in this book.

Trainee surveyors, c. 1900. Brecon photographer H. Hobbiss took this photograph of the surveyors and their theodolites in a garden in the town near the present Co-op.